Editor

Eric Migliaccio

Editor in Chief

Ina Massler Levin, M.A.

Creative Director

Karen J. Goldfluss, M.S. Ed.

Illustrator

Clint McKnight

Cover Artist

Brenda DiAntonis

Art Coordinator

Renée Christine Yates

Imaging

James Edward Grace

Publisher

Mary D. Smith, M.S. Ed.

Us...

Writer's Notebook

A Place of Their Own Where Students Can...

COLLECT THEIR IDEAS

DISCOVER THEIR VOICE

LEARN TO LIVE LIKE WRITERS

Includes Standards & Benchmarks

Author

Jane Webster, M.Ed.

Teacher Created Resources, Inc.

6421 Industry Way
Westminster, CA 92683
www.teachercreated.com

ISBN: 978-1-4206-2577-6

© 2010 Teacher Created Resources, Inc.
Made in U.S.A.

Teacher Created Resources

Table of Contents

Introduction

The Writer's Notebook and
Its Place in the Writing Curriculum

Often times, when a writing assignment is given in class, hands immediately shoot up and students nervously ask those same three familiar questions:

- ✏ "How long does it have to be?"
- ✏ "When is it due?"
- ✏ "Are we being graded on it?"

When teachers hear these responses over and over again, they come to realize that their young writers have become nothing more than task-completers. This type of unmotivated writer speeds through assignments and produces writing that lacks both voice and imagination. Thoughtfully added details that would have created vivid word pictures and interesting facts that would have adequately explained ideas are omitted for the sake of just getting it done. Precise, more-descriptive vocabulary is not present because these students don't want to waste time looking for the appropriate words. No voice is evident because they have not taken the time to reflect on the assigned topic and added their own personal memories and opinions that would have given their writing a "heartbeat." In short, their writing is lifeless. Sound familiar?

This, then, is why every writing program must offer the opportunity for students to have access to a Writer's Notebook. These small notebooks will become invaluable companions as students learn to use them effectively when they write. They will become the go-to place when they need to retrieve a memory or some piece of factual information to inspire or enrich a piece of writing. They will learn to rely on them as a special place to capture cherished memories, conversations with interesting people, or ideas that warrant reflection. Colorful words and phrases that are collected in their notebooks will help to make their writing pieces sparkle with energetic vocabulary and beautiful, expressive figurative language.

The Writer's Notebook is a safe place for students to write. Since these are never graded, less-confident writers and/or writers with emerging second-language skills have a private place to try out new vocabulary words, practice expressing their ideas without ridicule or judgment, or simply enjoy the shear beauty and flow of written language. As students take the time to record their ideas, they will also learn to pay closer attention to their world. They will question why and how, make connections, and form opinions—all of which will be reflected in their writing as their voice becomes evident.

The lessons in this book will help you introduce third- and fourth-grade students to the practice of keeping a Writer's Notebook. However, as always, modeling this practice will have the most impact. If students observe how you reach for your notebook when you need to jot down an observation or record the events of some activity, they'll begin to do the same. Together you'll become a classroom of real writers as you use this precious resource to produce stunning pieces of literature. Writer's Notebooks come to be cherished friends over time, and students will often save notebooks from past years to retrieve ideas from them. Thus, keeping a Writer's Notebook helps to ensure a lifelong love of writing. What a wonderful gift to give to our students.

The 6 + 1 Traits of Writing

Using a Writer's Notebook supports each of the 6 + 1 Traits of Writing in the following ways:

✏ **Ideas** *(Lessons 1–6, 8, 10–16, 18)*

Writer's Notebooks provide students with a place to record all of the random thoughts and observations they might need later to inspire or energize a piece of writing. Ideas might come from their collected poems, quotes, or various lists. Bits of overheard conversations or poignant memories of amazing people might be retrieved to add critical details.

✏ **Organization** *(Lessons 1–6, 14)*

Organization skills are refined as students collect their ideas and informally arrange them chronologically or in order of importance. Students may later cross out what they deem useless, rearrange as logic dictates, or highlight those main ideas that they want to be heard loud and clear. Formerly forgotten details may be squeezed in between lines at the appropriate places, and the chunking of similar ideas into paragraphs may be evident as new ideas are added.

✏ **Voice** *(Lessons 7–12, 14, 15)*

A Writer's Notebook provides young writers with the perfect, private place to try out their voice without fear of ridicule. They are able to loudly express their anger or cry through their words, and they are free to rejoice and celebrate using the language they know best. As confidence builds, they begin to take risks by revealing more and more of themselves through their writing. In short, their voice explodes from between the pages of their Writer's Notebook and finally goes public.

✏ **Word Choice** *(Lessons 11, 15)*

Having a special place to copy interesting words and examples of figurative language is invaluable to any writer but more so to early language learners and anyone who struggles with vocabulary. The Writer's Notebook provides a home to the idioms, similes, metaphors, and colloquialisms that enliven writing. It is a jewelry box for selecting the proper gem to put in a piece of writing.

✏ **Sentence Fluency** *(Lesson 15)*

Although a Writer's Notebook is not intended to contain complete, fully crafted pieces of writing, it is where especially descriptive phrases, quotes, and precise vocabulary are stored to create lyrical sentences that flow together like music. As students reread their entries, they'll notice the short, choppy sounds of their quick notations and realize that revisions will be needed to effectively express their ideas.

✏ **Conventions** *(Lesson 4)*

This safe "No-Red-Pen Zone" allows ideas to reign supreme and conventions to step aside, at least for a while. However, many writers use their notebooks to generate lists of troublesome spelling demons and useful punctuation rules. Some even include samples of dialogue punctuation and commas at work to help with editing later on.

✏ **Presentation** *(Lessons 1, 6, 10)*

A Writer's Notebook may often hold ideas for dramatic, comic, or even mysterious presentation of writing pieces. Clippings, sketches, graphs and charts, and artistic fonts and flourishes all add drama to writing. It allows young writers to add the big "Ta-dah!" to their published work.

Standards Correlation Chart

The activities in this book meet the following third- and fourth-grade Language Arts standards, which are used with permission from McREL. (Copyright 2006 McREL. Mid-continent Research for Education and Learning. Address: 4601 DTC Boulevard, Suite 500, Denver, CO 80237. Telephone: 303-377-0990. Website: www.mcrel.org/standards-benchmarks.)

Standards and Benchmarks	Lesson Number(s)
Standard 1. Uses the general skills and strategies of the writing process	
1. Prewriting: Uses prewriting strategies to plan written work	1, 3–6, 8, 12–16
2. Drafting and Revising: Uses strategies to draft and revise written work	7, 9, 14
3. Editing and Publishing: Uses strategies to edit and publish written work	6, 10
4. Evaluates own and others' writing	3, 4, 7–9, 17, 18
5. Uses strategies to write for different audiences	11, 14
6. Uses strategies to write for a variety of purposes	1, 2, 4, 5, 11, 12, 14, 16, 17
7. Writes expository compositions	8
8. Writes narrative accounts, such as poems or stories	4, 14
9. Writes autobiographical compositions	1, 6, 10
10. Writes expressive compositions	8, 9, 11, 12, 14, 16, 19
11. Writes in response to literature	4, 15, 17
12. Writes personal letters	14
Standard 2. Uses the stylistic and rhetorical aspects of writing	
1. Uses descriptive language that clarifies and enhances ideas	7, 11, 12, 14–16
2. Uses paragraph form in writing	6
Standard 3. Uses grammatical and mechanical conventions in written compositions	
3. Uses nouns in written compositions	10
5. Uses adjectives in written compositions	9
Standard 8. Uses listening and speaking strategies for different purposes	
1. Contributes to group discussions	2, 4–9, 11–13, 17, 19
2. Asks questions in class	2, 8
3. Responds to questions and comments	2, 4, 5, 7–9, 12–15
4. Listens to classmates and adults	1–20
6. Uses level appropriate vocabulary in speech	11
7. Makes oral presentations to class	1, 11, 19
11. Listens for specific information in spoken texts	8, 11, 19
12. Understands that language reflects different regions and cultures	7, 11

Assembling the Writer's Notebooks

Teachers might choose to purchase (or have students purchase) a spiral-bound notebook to use exclusively as their Writer's Notebook, but spiral-bound notebooks present several potential problems. First of all, students get in the habit of tearing out pages when they run out of filler paper, and before you know it, they're asking for another notebook. Second, for some reason, students seem to "lose" them in their desks because they look like every other notebook. Also, over time the metal spirals "mysteriously" start working their way out of position and can cause injury. And last and most importantly, an average-looking spiral-bound notebook just doesn't seem quite special enough to be something so important and personal as a Writer's Notebook.

What does seem to work best are Writer's Notebooks that are assembled. They are . . .

- ✏ convenient for students to locate in their desks
- ✏ relatively easy and quick to assemble
- ✏ very easy to personalize
- ✏ inexpensive to make with common, available materials
- ✏ appropriate for many grade levels
- ✏ not usually a victim of torn-out pages
- ✏ just the right size to be special

Materials Needed:

To assemble the notebooks, you will need only three things: plain manila file folders, copy paper (10 sheets per notebook), and a saddle (or long neck) stapler.

Assembly Directions:

For each notebook use a paper cutter to cut a 6" x 9" section from the folded side of a manila file folder. Next, count out 10 sheets of plain copy paper and fold them in half. Then, using a saddle stapler, attach the pages inside the manila cover with two staples. This will make a durable Writer's Notebook with 40 pages for writing, usually enough for the entire school year.

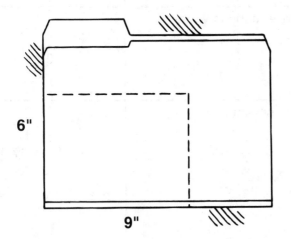
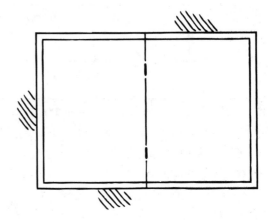

Notes:

- ✏ Don't throw away the leftover folder scraps. See Lesson 14 (page 46) for recycling ideas.
- ✏ If time and/or available resources are a real issue, Writer's Notebooks can be assembled using regular filler notebook paper inside a folder with center brads. This alternative type of notebook, although not ideal because of its size, is better than students not having one at all. After all, the focus is on the ideas, not the notebook itself.

Chapter 1

Helping Students Collect Their Ideas

Introduction

Take a look inside your students' desks and you will quickly discover that organization is sometimes not the strength of many of our third- and fourth-grade writers. That being said, it's up to us to help them arrange their ideas in a Writer's Notebook so that they are easily retrievable when needed to inspire or enliven a piece of writing.

Almost every household has a special place, dubbed by family members as "the junk drawer," where useful odds and ends seem to accumulate. It may hold batteries, receipts, coupons, newspaper and magazine clippings, appliance warranties, pizza-delivery menus, scissors, miscellaneous business cards, a flashlight, rubber bands, twist ties—you name it! To some people, this type of storage system would seem chaotic, but it's really an organized chaos. Family members may have to rummage around a bit to find what they're looking for, but they know that if they are persistent, they'll be able to pull out exactly what they need when they need it. In short, a junk drawer does not really hold junk.

This is the essence of a Writer's Notebook. It is a special place to collect "useful odds and ends" that can be retrieved when needed. It is the go-to place for ideas great and small. It is the salvation when a bad case of writer's block occurs. Writers may have to "rummage around a bit" to find what it is they are is looking for, but it will be there because that is where they placed it for safekeeping.

As you begin the process of introducing the Writer's Notebook to your students, it is imperative that you encourage their early attempts at storing away their ideas, and you must regularly take advantage of opportunities to model the stashing away of your own thoughts in your "junk drawer," as well. More importantly, students need to regularly observe you retrieving an idea when you have need of it. That way its function in the writing process will be reinforced and students will come to depend on their Writer's Notebooks as loyal writing companions, as well.

For most third- and fourth-grade students, writing instruction through the primary grades focused on "proper" writing. They were taught and expected to spell words correctly, use complete sentences with proper capitalization and punctuation, and demonstrate accepted rules of grammar when producing written assignments. Most likely, too, they were introduced somewhere along the way to the idea of journaling. Teachers may have provided students with some type of notebook in which to respond to a daily prompt, usually completed by the class all at the same time. While this activity did allow students to express their ideas and did plant the seeds of creative writing, it still remained a structured writing assignment. This, then, is why the introduction of the Writer's Notebook at these two grade levels is so crucial at this stage of their writing development. These seem to be the pivotal years, when they'll either begin to fight writing tooth and nail or learn to actually look forward to expressing their ideas on paper. Such a responsibility you have! Make the most of each lesson to share your love of the craft of writing, and soon you'll begin to see that same love emerge in your students.

Lesson 1 – Personalizing the Writer's Notebook

When you first introduce Writer's Notebooks, it is crucial that your students immediately feel a strong sense of ownership and oneness with their new possession. To do this, have students personalize their notebooks by designing unique covers that reveal something about them.

Materials Needed: *Writer's Notebook, colored pencils and/or crayons*

1. Begin by briefly introducing the Writer's Notebook. Tell your students that they will be using these all year long as a special place to record their ideas, memories, and feelings. Explain that many famous authors use a Writer's Notebook to save ideas that they may want to include in their stories.

2. Explain that, first of all, each of their Writer's Notebooks needs to be personalized. Distribute the blank notebooks. Instruct students to write "My Writer's Notebook," "[Name]'s Writer's Notebook," or some other appropriate title on the cover. Write some of these choices on the board for them to copy. Their name must go on the cover. Encourage students to use their best handwriting.

3. Next, have students draw five or six pictures of objects or people that are very important to them at this point in their lives. Ahead of time, design your own cover. Take a few moments to explain the pictures that you chose to draw and tell why each is important to you. Stress thoughtfulness as they make their own selections. Also, use the opportunity to show how you worked carefully to make your cover neat and attractive.

4. Give students plenty of time to complete their covers. Colored pencils or crayons work best for coloring in the pictures. Discourage (or forbid) the use of markers and/or glitter glue, since these can often produce messy, unattractive results. Encourage neatness so that your students will be proud of their new writing companions all year long. (See page 9 for examples of completed covers.)

5. When students are finished, have them pair up and take turns explaining their picture choices to their partners. This is a *very important* first step in the process of sharing a bit of themselves as writers.

6. Last, ask your students to select one of the pictures from their Writer's Notebook cover. Then, have them turn to their first page and write a few lines about why that one thing or person is so important to them. Model this first with one of your cover pictures. Read your entry, then give your students a few minutes to complete their own.

7. Some students may be eager to share what they wrote, so allow time for them to do so. Do not make anyone read who seems hesitant. Confidence in the worth of their ideas and their willingness to share them with people they trust will come later.

8. Have students store their Writer's Notebooks in their desks in an area where they will be easy to locate and will stay reasonably safe from damage.

Lesson 1 – Personalizing the Writer's Notebook (cont.)

Lesson 2 – Establishing Classroom Guidelines

Once the Writer's Notebooks have been distributed and personalized, classroom guidelines need to be set in place so that students will feel comfortable writing entries and storing them when not in use.

Materials Needed: *a transparency of page 11*

1. Explain that for Writer's Notebooks to be effective, certain guidelines for their use need to be established in the classroom. Create a transparency of "The Writer's Notebook Classroom Contract" (page 11) and together develop the rules for use. Later, transfer these ideas onto a poster to be displayed in the classroom.

   You may want to include these conditions as part of your contract:

   I, your **Teacher**, promise to . . .

   1. respect your privacy and not read your notebook unless you give me permission.

   2. never show your notebook to other individuals without your permission.

   3. allow you to write as needed without penalty unless you have been given other work to complete first.

   4. not assign a grade to your Writer's Notebook.

   We, your **Students**, promise to . . .

   1. keep our Writer's Notebooks in our desks and not take them home.

   2. make entries only when you ask us to or when we have free time to do so.

   3. never read another person's notebook unless given permission.

   4. treat our Writer's Notebooks carefully and not tear out pages or use them for doodling.

   ---

2. Remind your students again that they need to take good care of these notebooks because they are to last for the entire school year. Inform your students that you'll be occasionally checking to see if they are indeed writing in their notebooks. You will do this by quickly flipping though through them—without reading their words, of course. This gentle warning should be enough to motivate negligent students to get writing. Plan to do this for the first time in a week or two so that students who haven't been using their notebooks will begin to make regular entries.

3. Students may ask some "What if?" questions. As a class, decide answers to the following:

   ✐ "What if I lose my notebook?"

   ✐ "What if I have an idea at home? Where do I write it down?"

   ✐ "What if I fill up my notebook before the end of the year?"

   For future reference, record any decisions that are made.

Lesson 2 – Establishing Classroom Guidelines (cont.)

The Writer's Notebook Classroom Contract

I, your **Teacher**, promise to . . .

1. _____

   _____

2. _____

   _____

3. _____

   _____

4. _____

   _____

We, your **Students**, promise to . . .

1. _____

   _____

2. _____

   _____

3. _____

   _____

4. _____

   _____

Lesson 3 – Writing Entries

Most often, ideas are entered into the Writer's Notebook as they come to mind. That's why writers need to keep their notebook and a pencil always handy.

Materials Needed: *a transparency of the sample entry on page 13*

1. Explain that entries in a Writer's Notebook are written in a special way.

Entries are . . .

- ✏ usually just a few lines long
- ✏ separated from each other by a dividing line
- ✏ most often dated
- ✏ written on both the fronts and backs of pages

Entries don't have to . . .

- ✏ be written in complete sentences
- ✏ contain perfect spelling or punctuation
- ✏ be written with perfect handwriting (just readable handwriting)

2. Remind students that these are just their quick notations—not complete pieces of writing—so short, concise entries will serve them best. Only enough needs to be written to spark a memory. Use an example from your own entries. For example, if you went to see a Fourth of July parade, your entry may have looked like this:

> 4th of July Parade, 2008, really great floats, kids scared of loud fire engine sirens, felt patriotic when soldiers marched by, lump in throat.

Point out that you didn't use complete sentences or perfect handwriting, but you were able to save your most important ideas by using just enough words to spark your memory about the event. (Make a transparency of page 13 to show as an example.)

3. Now make sure students understand the word *chronological*. It means "in time order." For most writers this is the most natural way to make entries. It is writing down what's on your mind as thoughts come to you. All types of entries are intermixed on the pages, and sometimes they are dated for reference. Explain to students that on some days they will have many ideas to record, but on other days nothing will be written. (Refer again to the transparency to illustrate this.)

4. Remind students not to crowd their notebook entries. For instance, if they were creating a list of all the times they felt proud of themselves, they should leave a little space before drawing a line so that they can add more later.

5. Some teachers prefer setting a time aside each day for students to write in their notebooks. This is a bit unnatural since inspiration comes at different times to each student, and students may end up writing useless words just because they are told that this is their time to write. This defeats the whole purpose of the Writer's Notebook and becomes just another routine classroom assignment.

Lesson 3 – Writing Entries (cont.)

Sample Entry

6/8 Saw a SHOOTING STAR — Look up legends about them and write a folktale.

6/9 ANIMAL PLANET — Said Walruses have "rubbery lips". Sounds funny!

Small Things That Are FRUSTRATING/ANNOYING:
- Dead battery
- A Splinter
- Missing button
- Stain on favorite shirt
- Pebble in my shoe
- Mosquito bites
- Wrong Numbers
- Broken pencil tip

British Words from HARRY POTTER and the
                          Half-Blood Prince:
- Snogging (p. 117)
- Taking the Mickey (p. 190)
- Going Spare (p. 63)
- Gone 'round the Twist (p. 83)
- Nutter (p. 332)
- Tot-up (p. 148)

(Use these in a story about new neighbors from England.)

6/11 GRANDPA'S BIRTHDAY PARTY — He let us open his presents 'cause he said he liked to watch us. Mom said it's arthritis (He never complains.)

Lesson 4 – What Goes in a Writer's Notebook?

A Writer's Notebook is a safe place for budding authors to practice, develop, and reflect on the world around them. Just to give students a notebook and to tell them to make entries is not enough. Young writers need to be taught how to reflect and record their ideas in one place.

Materials Needed: *a jewelry box with jewelry, a packet of seeds, a full junk drawer (maybe from your desk at school), a light bulb, a transparency of page 16, and student copies of pages 17–18 (the columns on page 17 should be cut apart)*

1. Explain that a Writer's Notebook is a special place to save ideas for writing. You may wish to compare it to a jewelry box that holds writing "gems," a seed packet that holds "seeds of ideas," or a junk drawer that contains "useful odds and ends."

    ✏ Show your students a jewelry box containing a few items of jewelry. Tell them that sometimes you (or a woman you know) like to look a little fancy, so you (or she) like to select an interesting necklace, bracelet, or earrings to make the outfit really sparkle. (Maybe you want to try some on for effect.) Tell students that a Writer's Notebook holds little "gem" words or phrases that can make their writing sparkle, too.

    ✏ Now hold up a packet of seeds. Tell students that gardeners plant seeds that will one day develop into lovely flowers or tasty vegetables. Explain that a Writer's Notebook is like the seed packet: it doesn't contain your completely developed ideas, just seeds of ideas. Later, these seeds of ideas will help produce beautiful, fully developed details when they are "planted" in your writing.

    ✏ Lastly, produce a junk drawer, most likely from your desk at school. Show the contents to your students and explain that this drawer is where you stash "stuff" when you're in a hurry. (Be sure to show a variety of objects and explain why each one is important to you and not really junk at all.) Explain that when you need that object, you know right where to go to get it. You may have to scoot things around and dig a little, but you know it's in there somewhere. Now compare the Writer's Notebook to your junk drawer. Tell them that their notebooks are for collecting little odds and ends that are important to them—and when they need that quote, fancy word, or memory, they'll know right where to go to get it.

2. Explain that since we all now know what a Writer's Notebook is for, we need to think about what "seeds," "gems," or "odds and ends" should be collected in them. Ask your students what an *idea* is. Record their suggestions on the board. Here are some possible answers: something your brain makes, something that just pops into your head, a thought about something, something you see or read that you want to think about later.

3. Hold up a light bulb. Tell students that sometimes in cartoon strips, the cartoonist will draw a light bulb over a character's head to show that he or she has had an idea. Show an example of such a cartoon if you have one. Explain that our Writer's Notebooks are for light-bulb storage, as well. (You might want to use the light bulb later as a prop. For fun, hold it above your head whenever you have an idea that needs to go in your Writer's Notebook.)

Lesson 4 – What Goes In a Writer's Notebook? (cont.)

4. Make a transparency of the large version of "What's in a Writer's Notebook?" (page 16). Use it to lead a discussion about each of the entry ideas. Together, try to add more to the list. Hang a poster in the classroom so that students can add even more.

5. Make copies of the smaller versions of "What's in a Writer's Notebook?" (page 17) on bright paper, cut them apart, and have students tape these inside the front cover of their Writer's Notebooks. These will serve as a resource to suggest ideas when they get "stuck."

6. Stories from the basal reader or books read aloud to the whole class often provide ideas. Make it a point to ask your students, "Did any ideas pop into your head after reading/hearing this story? Could you use any of these in your own writing?" Most often, students will be inspired by the interesting characters, and they'll want to write about a knight or a two-headed giant, too. Encourage students to write an entry into their Writer's Notebook as soon as possible so they won't forget the details. Remind them to use descriptive words or draw pictures, if needed.

7. On selected occasions—like right after an especially interesting school assembly or field trip—set aside a few minutes for all of you to quickly jot down your reactions to what you just saw or heard. Later, assign this as a writing topic so that students will see the value in quickly storing away ideas while their memories of an event are still fresh.

8. This is the perfect opportunity to share a few of the entries you've been making in your own Writer's Notebook. Make sure you select a variety of ideas as examples. Share a quote that you recently heard or read, a short inspirational poem, a memory of an important event, an interesting new word you'd like to use sometime, a list you've created, or a website you recently came across that would be a good resource for background information on a subject.

9. Distribute copies of "Writer's Notebook Topics from A–Z" (page 18) to spark some ideas. If you wish, you may ask students to create their own A-Z list, too. These lists can be kept in the students' notebooks.

10. Allow plenty of time after this lesson for students to begin collecting ideas for their notebooks. Some ideas may be really "out there," but accept them all and praise the students for their efforts. First-time keepers of Writer's Notebooks tend to value quantity over quality. More-experienced writers, however, save only bits and pieces of their thoughts and observations that they consider meaningful and useful for possible writing projects. At times, you might ask a student, "How do you plan to include this idea [quote, poem, anecdote] in your writing?" Never ask them to erase what they have written—that's for them to decide. However, by posing this question, it will encourage students to evaluate each entry as to whether it's potentially useful or just filler.

11. Remind students to use all five senses to collect ideas. Encourage them to look around and take in the interesting details of their surroundings. Ask students to write down examples of new or interesting things they have recently heard, seen, smelled, tasted, or touched. These notations might inspire others in the classroom.

Lesson 4 – What Goes in a Writer's Notebook? (cont.)

What's in a Writer's Notebook?

- important events you want to remember

- interesting facts about people you've met

- family stories or traditions

- dreams you've had

- new words or expressions that you want to try in your own writing

- lists of all kinds

- times that you've been happy, angry, scared, excited, worried, disappointed, etc.

- conversations

- famous quotes that are meaningful to you

- book reviews

- descriptions of people, places, etc.

- current events that concern you

- special poems that you like

- ideas for stories

- jokes or riddles

- reflections or memories about anything

- other ideas: _____

- _____

- _____

Lesson 4 – What Goes in a Writer's Notebook? (cont.)

What's in a Writer's Notebook?

- important events you want to remember
- interesting facts about people you've met
- family stories or traditions
- dreams you've had
- new words or expressions that you want to try in your own writing
- lists of all kinds
- times that you've been happy, angry, scared, excited, disappointed, etc.
- conversations
- famous quotes that are meaningful to you
- book reviews
- descriptions of people, places, etc.
- current events that concern you
- special poems that you like
- ideas for stories
- jokes or riddles
- reflections or memories about anything
- other ideas: _____ _____ _____ _____

What's in a Writer's Notebook?

- important events you want to remember
- interesting facts about people you've met
- family stories or traditions
- dreams you've had
- new words or expressions that you want to try in your own writing
- lists of all kinds
- times that you've been happy, angry, scared, excited, disappointed, etc.
- conversations
- famous quotes that are meaningful to you
- book reviews
- descriptions of people, places, etc.
- current events that concern you
- special poems that you like
- ideas for stories
- jokes or riddles
- reflections or memories about anything
- other ideas: _____ _____ _____ _____

What's in a Writer's Notebook?

- important events you want to remember
- interesting facts about people you've met
- family stories or traditions
- dreams you've had
- new words or expressions that you want to try in your own writing
- lists of all kinds
- times that you've been happy, angry, scared, excited, disappointed, etc.
- conversations
- famous quotes that are meaningful to you
- book reviews
- descriptions of people, places, etc.
- current events that concern you
- special poems that you like
- ideas for stories
- jokes or riddles
- reflections or memories about anything
- other ideas: _____ _____ _____ _____

Lesson 4 – What Goes in a Writer's Notebook? *(cont.)*

Writer's Notebook Topics from A to Z

A – Tell about an <u>animal</u> encounter.

B – What things <u>bother</u> you?

C – What <u>compliments</u> have you received or given lately?

D – Tell about some <u>dreams</u> you've had.

E – What can you never get <u>enough</u> of?

F – Tell all about your <u>family</u>.

G – Describe your <u>grandparents</u>.

H – Who is your <u>hero</u>? Why?

I – Describe your favorite <u>ice cream</u> flavor.

J – What is the funniest <u>joke</u> you've ever heard?

K – Tell about some ways you can be <u>kind</u> to others.

L – Tell about something that you <u>lost</u>.

M – What things make you really <u>mad</u>?

N – What <u>noises</u> do you love or hate to hear?

O – Give your <u>opinion</u> about several important issues.

P – If you could spend 15 minutes alone with the <u>principal</u>, what would you talk about?

Q – What <u>questions</u> would you like to ask the president?

R – What <u>rules</u> would you like to change at school?

S – Tell about a <u>scar</u> that you have. Where is it located? How did you get it?

T – Tell about the last <u>time</u> you got in trouble.

U – Tell about a very <u>unusual</u> day.

V – Where would you like to go on a <u>vacation</u>? What would you do there?

W – Make a list of everything that <u>wiggles</u>.

X – If a doctor took an <u>x-ray</u> of your brain, what would he see?

Y – What do you think you'll remember most about this <u>year</u> at school?

Z – What would you like to have <u>zero</u> of?

Lesson 5 – Creating Resource Lists of All Kinds

Lists are a convenient and space-saving way to organize items that a person wants to remember. A Writer's Notebook is a perfect place for writers to make lists of all sorts of things.

Materials Needed: *transparencies of pages 20–21 and a copy of* Charlotte's Web *by E.B. White*

1. Make a transparency of "What Do I Need at the Grocery Store?" (page 20). Tell students that recently you went to the grocery store after writing down all the things that you needed to buy. Show them Samples A and B. Ask them which one would be easier for you to use at the grocery store. They'll choose Sample B, of course. Discuss why. Reasons might be that Sample A is too wordy, making the items harder to find quickly; bigger paper would be needed on which to write Sample A; and Sample A would be harder to cross off the items as you put them in your cart.

2. Explain that a Writer's Notebook is the perfect place to keep lists of all kinds. These lists can corral special words or ideas to create descriptions, categorize ideas or feelings, or spark memories. Together as a class, create "A List of Lists" (page 21) on the overhead projector. Your lists might include:

   - feelings—times you felt really happy (or disappointed, scared, nervous, proud, etc.)
   - holiday or seasonal words
   - idioms, similes, or colloquialisms you would like to use in your writing
   - favorite characters in books
   - things that are scary, disgusting, soft, fragrant, delicious, etc.
   - colorful adjectives
   - places you would like to visit
   - famous people you would like to meet
   - movies you have seen
   - sports words, math words, superhero words, etc.
   - topics you would like to write about
   - unusual words

   (If you wish, make copies of the completed "A List of Lists" for students to use as a resource, or transfer the information to a classroom poster for all to see.)

3. If students have read *Charlotte's Web,* they will remember how E.B. White incorporates long lists of foods that Templeton the rat eats throughout the story. (Cite several examples.) Ask students why they think the author did this even though it wasn't necessary to the story line. It could have been to add humor, to better describe Templeton's character, or just to make the story more interesting. Challenge your students to try this strategy in their writing some time.

4. Now ask students to select one list from "A List of Lists" and collect examples in their Writer's Notebook. For example, if a student selects "Idioms," he might list "a frog in my throat," "so hungry I could eat a horse," "I put my foot in my mouth," etc. Remind students to leave a little space before drawing the separation line so that more items can be added to the list later. As always, if the occasion arises, model your use of one of your Writer's Notebook lists to supply an idea or detail for writing.

Lesson 5 – Creating Resource Lists of All Kinds (cont.)

What Do I Need at the Grocery Store?

Sample A

I need a lot of things today. First of all, I need a loaf of wheat bread and some hamburger buns; and while I'm in the bread section, I should probably pick up a package of donuts for Sunday morning. Next, I can't forget to buy a box of graham crackers and some marshmallow crème to go with them. Also, I think I'm out of frozen corn and frozen mixed vegetables, so I should get those too and maybe a half gallon of vanilla ice cream would be nice for dessert tonight. A jar of hot fudge sauce would make it really special. Last, I probably should buy more paper towels and glass cleaner since I need to wash windows this weekend. I guess that's it.

Sample B

Grocery List

wheat bread

frozen mixed vegetables

hamburger buns

vanilla ice cream

donuts

hot fudge sauce

graham crackers

paper towels

marshmallow crème

glass cleaner

frozen corn

Lesson 5 – Creating Resource Lists of All Kinds (cont.)

A List of Lists

What lists could we collect?

_____   _____

_____   _____

_____   _____

_____   _____

_____   _____

_____   _____

_____   _____

_____   _____

_____   _____

_____   _____

Lesson 6 – A Place for Pictures, Clippings, and Sketches

Sometimes a picture *is* worth a thousand words. Collecting a few pictures can serve as inspirational visual cues. A picture of a castle in Bavaria might inspire a fairy tale, or a sample of Chinese writing may prompt a young writer to copy his or her haiku using that script style.

Materials Needed: *small business envelopes (one per student)*

1. Although a Writer's Notebook isn't meant to be a scrapbook, sometimes writers need visual cues to help stimulate ideas. Here are some ideas of visuals to add to the notebooks. You should remind students to add only those that they feel are really useful, and occasionally they should cull their collection so their notebooks won't be too bulky.

   Students might want to collect these items:

   - examples of fancy script, artistic fonts, or flourishes
   - pictures of interesting people and places to be used as story starters or for description
   - newspaper or magazine articles with interesting facts
   - clip-art or other computer-generated images

2. Provide a small business envelope to be taped to the inside back cover of their Writer's Notebook to hold these resources.

3. To practice using visual cues for writing, select an interesting picture from the basal reader. Briefly talk about it, then tell your students that it has inspired you to make a connection—one that you'd like to write about. (For example, if it's a picture of cowboys around a campfire, tell your students that it has inspired you to write about the first time you built a campfire when your family went camping.) Now have them browse through their readers to find a picture that might spark a connection. Have them write a short paragraph about that topic. Share responses in small groups or as a whole class.

4. For students who are visual learners, having the ability—and even the encouragement—to collect images as inspirational resources will be invaluable; and for ESL students, pictures will serve as a springboard for generating new vocabulary. Remember to remind these students often to keep collecting visuals to serve as writing prompts.

Chapter 2

Encouraging Students to Find Their Voice

Introduction

Although there is definitely a place for formal encyclopedia-type writing, this is not what we hope to see in writing pieces created by our students. We want writing that is alive. We want to be able to feel the author's heartbeat and hear the voice of a real person explaining real ideas with a real genuineness and style.

Students spend most of the school day reading and studying content-area textbooks that are devoid of voice. Voice has been squelched in order to present facts and information without distraction. It is no wonder then that students often create pieces of writing that mirror this type of "personalitylessness." Imagine how exciting a science or social studies textbook would be if students could experience content presented in less-formal language with an occasional exclamation, a bit of humor, or rich figurative language added to the text.

That being said, the very best gift that a teacher can give budding young writers is the permission to be themselves when they write—to use their voice. When students feel comfortable revealing their most personal memories and sharing their opinions and feelings, then their writing becomes real, and readers can sense right away that the author trusts them to receive these sincere revelations.

When scoring submitted writing pieces, teachers should always acknowledge the effective use of voice:

- ✏ "I hear you loud and clear!"
- ✏ "This writing speaks to me."
- ✏ "Message received!"
- ✏ "Your voice is evident."
- ✏ "I hear a real person talking!"

When students read original stories or personal narratives to the class, writing that contains voice should receive feedback like:

- ✏ "This really sounds like you."
- ✏ "It's easy to tell how you felt about this event."
- ✏ "You made us feel [sad, happy, etc.], too."
- ✏ "Your opinions really came through."
- ✏ "When you write, it's like how you talk."

It's not just third- and fourth-graders who want to be heard; all of us share that need. When we write, we are "talking on paper"; our pencil is moving, not our vocal chords, to make our voice heard. As writers, our earnest hope is that we find an audience who will be inspired, challenged, entertained, or comforted by our words.

Lesson 7 – Defining Voice

Materials Needed: *a transparency of page 26, student copies of page 27, large sheet of white construction paper, and markers*

1. Select a paragraph from a science, social studies, or math textbook and have students follow along as you read. When you are finished, ask them these questions:

   - Who wrote this paragraph?

   - Is it a man or a woman?

   - How old is this person?

   - What country is this person from?

   - How does this person feel about the subject matter?

   As you might predict, your students will not be able to answer these questions, but rather will just offer unsupported guesses. Explain to them that textbooks are written without "voice" so that readers don't hear the author but rather focus on the subject matter only.

2. Now explain that as writers we should write with "voice" to let our readers know that a real person is willing to share a part of him- or herself. We are saying, *This writing is "of me" because I'm revealing my . . .*

   - **(O) opinions**—how I feel about certain issues

   - **(F) feelings**—how I react

   - **(M) memories**—stories from my past

   - **(E) expressions**—the words I use to share my ideas

3. On the overhead, show the "Which One Has Voice?" transparency (page 26). Ask students to guess which paragraph has voice. In paragraph 2 (the correct answer), locate examples of opinions, feelings, memories, and expressions that illustrate "voice."

   Examples:

   - **opinions:** "noble turkey," "must have liked the bright colors," "seems really odd"

   - **feelings:** "I love bright colors too."

   - **memories:** "I've seen pictures . . ."

   - **expressions:** "Hey," "Go figure!"

   (Also emphasize that while both paragraphs give readers the same exact information, the second version makes it more interesting.)

4. Writing should sound like a real person wrote it, not a robot. The reader should sense the "heartbeat" of the writer. Let your students know that this is the type of writing that you expect from them. You expect to "hear" their heartbeat and their voice—not experience encyclopedia-type writing—when you read their writing.

Lesson 7 – Defining Voice (cont.)

5. Divide your class into small groups. Tell them that each group is going to be generating a list of "Voice Similes." Make sure that your students understand what a simile is by giving a few examples (e.g., "quick like a bunny," "as happy as a clam"). Now provide this pattern on the board or on an overhead:

    ✏   Writing without voice is like _____ without _____.

Now fill in the blanks to provide this example:

    ✏   Writing without voice is like a ___*cupcake*___ without ___*frosting*___.

Explain that even though cupcakes are good, frosting makes them even better. Ask your students for a few more examples. They might offer responses like:

    ✏   Writing without voice is like *a hot dog* without *mustard*.

    ✏   Writing without voice is like *Luke Skywalker* without *a light saber*.

    ✏   Writing without voice is like *a TV* without *a remote*.

    ✏   Writing without voice is like *a movie* without *popcorn*.

Distribute a "Voice Simile" worksheet (page 27) to each group. Allow time for each group to come up with 10 more similes. Encourage originality. (These can get really humorous.) Then instruct each group to select their favorite simile and write it at the bottom of their paper. Share the group favorites. If time allows, provide each group with a large piece of white construction paper and markers and have them design a VOICE poster using that simile.

Hang the posters around the classroom. Your students will soon realize the importance of voice to a piece of writing. It's that little bit extra that makes their writing come alive. Share the following thought (and tell your students that the little "extra" is voice):

> "The difference between *ordinary* and *extraordinary* is a little *extra*."
>   — *author unknown*

6. For an additional activity, copy a short paragraph from your students' science or social studies textbook. Put this paragraph on the top half of a page and make enough copies so that each student gets one. Then, instruct your students to rewrite the paragraph using their voice. Remind them that using their voice means that they should include their **o**pinions, **f**eelings, **m**emories, and **e**xpressions. (Display and review the example on page 26.)

7. Explain to your students that in the following lessons you'll be teaching them more about how to include their **o**pinions, **f**eelings, **m**emories, and unique **e**xpressions ("**of me**") in their writing and how to use their Writer's Notebook as a special place to collect these ideas.

Lesson 7 – Defining Voice (cont.)

Which One Has Voice?

paragraph 1

The wild turkey is native to North America. Many large flocks of these huge birds could be found roaming the forests long before the Pilgrims landed. These wild turkeys were an important source of food and clothing for many of the East Coast Native Americans, like the Wampanoag tribe who shared in that first Thanksgiving feast. Turkey feathers were also used in the construction of arrows.

paragraph 2

Hey, guess who came to America first, the turkeys or the Pilgrims? Yes, you're right! It was the noble turkey. Long before the Pilgrims served them to their guests (members of the Wampanoag tribe) at the first Thanksgiving feast, other Native Americans were already depending on them for food and even clothing. I've seen pictures of some of them wearing turkey feathers in their hair, so I guess they must have liked the bright colors. I love bright colors too. Also, they used turkey feathers to make arrows. That seems really odd, doesn't it? An arrow made with turkey feathers was used to kill turkeys. Go figure!

Lesson 7 – Defining Voice (cont.)

Voice Similes

Writing without **VOICE** is like _____ without _____

Writing without **VOICE** is like _____ without _____

Writing without **VOICE** is like _____ without _____

Writing without **VOICE** is like _____ without _____

Writing without **VOICE** is like _____ without _____

Writing without **VOICE** is like _____ without _____

Writing without **VOICE** is like _____ without _____

Writing without **VOICE** is like _____ without _____

Writing without **VOICE** is like _____ without _____

Here is our favorite one:

Writing without **VOICE** is like _____ without _____

Lesson 8 – Forming Opinions

Sometimes when we refer to someone as being highly opinionated, it's stated as a negative trait; it can mean that a certain person has a definite opinion on everything and forcefully shares those opinions, even without being asked.

Materials Needed: *an editorial page from a local newspaper, student copies of pages 30–31*

1. Discuss with your students the difference between facts and opinions. Facts are statements of what is true, what cannot be disputed. (Example: "Today is Monday.") Opinions are statements of belief, judgment, view, or feelings about something. (Example: "Mondays are the best!")

Provide a brief practice using these statements:

- All babies are cute. *(opinion)*
- There are seven days in a week. *(fact)*
- Dogs make the best pets. *(opinion)*
- Spinach is a leafy green vegetable. *(fact)*

- Our school is the best! *(opinion)*
- Area = length x width. *(fact)*
- Homework is unfair! *(opinion)*
- Riding a bicycle is easy. *(opinion)*

2. Explain to your students that when we write, our opinions about certain people, events, or issues often show through in what we write. It is one way that we show voice in our writing. Display the editorial page of your local newspaper. Explain that this is the page where people can express their opinions about certain happenings. Talk briefly about some of the topics that are discussed. Tell students that sometimes people write these articles to persuade others to hold the same view as they do; at other times, articles are printed just so opinions can be shared.

3. Explain that as writers we are expected to hold certain opinions about the world around us. (Writers can't be wishy-washy!) But what influences us to form opinions about important issues? On the board or overhead, create an idea web.

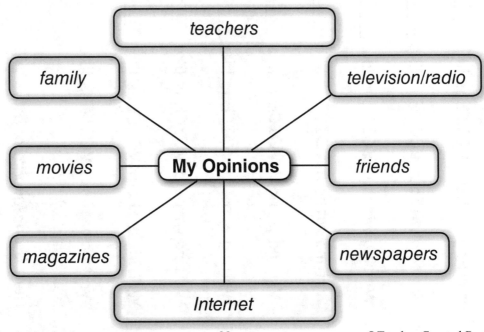

Lesson 8 – Forming Opinions (cont.)

4. Use "Expressing My Opinions" (page 30) as a way to help your students begin thinking about what opinions they hold on certain current issues. Instruct them to write two or three sentences about each topic. Afterwards, discuss some of their opinions. (Remind students that the opinions of others should be respected, even when they differ from the ones they themselves hold.)

5. Tell students that their Writer's Notebook should contain their honest opinions on many issues. At times, they may need to refer to these when doing persuasive writing pieces. From the "Expressing My Opinions" sheet, have students select three of the topics that they have the strongest opinions about and briefly record these opinions in their Writer's Notebook. A few weeks later, assign a persuasive essay and ask them to refer to their notebooks for a topic. Hopefully, they will appreciate the fact that they already had their opinions recorded somewhere ahead of time.

6. Although the following activity can get a little loud, it will help make your students more aware of the opinions of others while sharpening speaking and listening skills. Give each student a copy of "Connected by Our Opinions" (page 31). (Before making copies, write the name of each student, one per square.) Tell them that as writers we should be in touch with the opinions that others around us hold because, at times, we might want to address these in our writing. We can easily learn how people feel about certain issues by listening to them and sharing our viewpoints, as well.

Write several semi-controversial topics on the board. Here are a few suggestions:

- ✐ kids having cell phones
- ✐ eating junk food
- ✐ littering
- ✐ forming cliques at school
- ✐ borrowing money from friends

- ✐ year-round school
- ✐ being a tattletale
- ✐ watching PG-13 movies
- ✐ swearing
- ✐ getting paid to do chores at home

(You may also wish to add topics that are school specific, like a new school rule, etc. These topics might generate stronger opinions!)

Now instruct students to move around the room and find two people who share the same opinion on a given topic. They should connect the two names on the grid with a line, then fill in the sentences. For example:

_____Owen_____ and _____Jack_____ both ___don't borrow money from friends___.

_____Jennifer_____ and _____Matt_____ both ___think kids should get money for chores___.

After students have filled in their sheets, take time to discuss their findings. Were they surprised by the opinions that some students held on an issue? Did they agree or disagree with those opinions? Remind them that interactions with others turn conversation topics into thoughtful reflections in our Writer's Notebooks.

Lesson 8 – Forming Opinions (cont.)

Expressing My Opinions

What is my opinion of . . .

✎ school rules: _____

_____

✎ report cards: _____

_____

✎ doing chores at home: _____

_____

✎ watching television on school nights: _____

_____

✎ rules made by parents: _____

_____

✎ playing on sports teams: _____

_____

✎ the definition of a true friend: _____

_____

✎ homework on the weekends: _____

_____

✎ getting an allowance: _____

_____

✎ lying to make someone feel good: _____

_____

✎ sharing secrets with your friends: _____

_____

Lesson 8 – Forming Opinions (cont.)

Connected by Our Opinions

_____ and _____ both _____.

_____ and _____ both _____.

_____ and _____ both _____.

_____ and _____ both _____.

_____ and _____ both _____.

_____ and _____ both _____.

_____ and _____ both _____.

_____ and _____ both _____.

Lesson 9 – Getting in Touch with Feelings

Often when fledgling writers compose a personal narrative, they will forget to tell how they felt during the event. They forget that merely relating a story is not very interesting unless they can explain to the reader how an event or series of events affected them personally.

Materials Needed: transparencies of page 33–35, copies of page 35

1. Explain that good writers know that their writing becomes real when they put themselves into their work. Readers should be able to share the writer's emotions as they read along. Readers should be able to smile when a writer conveys his or her joy and get a little misty when they've been moved by the author's sorrow.

2. Make a transparency of "The Lost Pencil" story (page 33). Have a student read the story aloud. Ask what's missing. Hopefully, students will notice that the writer never shares his feelings about this frustrating event. Ask them to look for places to add "feeling" statements. Readers should be able to note that the writer's feelings changed throughout the story. (The corrected version on page 34 provides an example of where feeling statements could be added.)

3. This is a good opportunity to teach students how to add feeling statements in their writing. Some students get into the bad habit of simply tacking on a feeling statement at the end of a paragraph, like "I felt sad" or "I was so excited." Challenge your students to "Add On or Move It" (page 35) by rewriting the short paragraphs together as you model on the overhead. Using the first paragraph as an example, the idea is to do one of the following:

   ✏ **Add on** *to the ending feeling sentence:*
   Example: We were so excited because we wanted to try out the giant water slide.

   ✏ **Move it** *to somewhere inside the paragraph so it doesn't look tacked on:*
   Example: When we arrived at the hotel, we got to our room, unpacked our suitcases, and excitedly headed for the pool.

4. Tell students that it is very important that they are able to express their feelings when they write. The Writer's Notebook is a safe, private place where they can pour out their hearts without fear of others teasing them. Encourage students to write down their feelings often as situations arise. Encourage them to make use of precise adjectives to describe these feelings. As a resource, post a list of feeling words for students to use in their writing.

5. Model often how you have stored feeling statements in your Writer's Notebook. Read an entry that expresses how you felt about a certain event.

6. Have students search through their Writer's Notebooks to find an entry that stirs up a strong emotion. (Select one ahead of time. A positive feeling is probably best.) Divide the class into small groups. Ask one person in each group to read his or her entry and have the others carefully listen before commenting with questions, connections, or empathy. If there is time, encourage other students to share their entries. Monitor groups to make sure that all feelings are being respected.

Lesson 9 – Getting in Touch with Feelings (cont.)

The Lost Pencil

At school last Friday I lost my favorite mechanical pencil. I had always considered it my lucky pencil because once I took a spelling test with it and got 100%.

That morning, I remember loaning it to the girl behind me because she needed the eraser. I also remember putting it in my desk just before lunchtime.

However, when we came back from lunch, I opened my desk to get it for a math quiz, but it wasn't there.

I looked all over for it. I asked my friends if they had seen it. I even asked my teacher, but she had not seen it either. She looked in the wastebasket for my pencil, and I checked all through my desk for a second time. It was still lost.

Just before we went home, I looked all through my desk a third time. I even emptied it, but I couldn't find my lucky mechanical pencil. Maybe I never will. I guess it really wasn't so lucky for me, was it?

Lesson 9 – Getting in Touch with Feelings (cont.)

The Lost Pencil

I was so mad because my Dad had given it to me.

At school last Friday I lost my favorite mechanical pencil. ∧ I had always

considered it my lucky pencil because once I took a spelling test with it and

was thrilled to get

~~get~~ 100%.
∧

that I was feeling generous and loaned

That morning, I remember ~~loaning~~ it to the girl behind me because
∧

she needed the eraser. I also remember putting it in my desk just before

lunchtime.

However, when we came back from lunch, I opened my desk to get it for a

math quiz, but it wasn't there.

desperately

I looked all over for it. I asked my friends if they had seen it. I even asked
∧

my teacher, but she had not seen it either. She looked in the wastebasket

for my pencil, and I checked all through my desk for a second time. It was

still lost, *and I wanted to cry.*

hopefully

Just before we went home, I looked all through my desk a third time. I
∧

sadly

even emptied it, but I couldn't find my lucky mechanical pencil. Maybe I
∧

never will. I guess it really wasn't so lucky for me, was it?

Lesson 9 – Getting in Touch with Feelings *(cont.)*

Add On or Move It

Time to eliminate those dangling feeling statements . . .

1. When we arrived at the hotel, we got to our room, unpacked our suitcases, and headed for the pool. We were excited.

_____

_____

_____

2. A few weeks ago Dad had to take our dog Jasper to the animal hospital. He had been limping for a week. I felt worried.

_____

_____

_____

3. One day that I will never forget was the day I broke my arm. I broke it while playing soccer at my uncle's birthday party. I felt upset.

_____

_____

_____

4. Tomorrow I have a dental appointment. I need to have a tooth pulled before I can get my braces put on. I feel nervous.

_____

_____

_____

Lesson 10 – Saving Treasured Memories

Explain to your students that you are very old and that you've done a lot of things and met a lot of people in your very long life so far. Calculate the number of days you have lived. (Expect a loud reaction!) Then, explain that each day is a brand new opportunity for writers to experience the world around them and record significant events in their Writer's Notebook.

Materials Needed: *a transparency of page 37, small booklets made with half sheets of construction paper as covers with copy-paper pages stapled inside*

1. Explain that some authors and other famous people write their memoirs. Write the word *memoirs* on the board and ask what other word it looks like (i.e., *memory*). Explain that memoirs are a collection of memories about his or her life that a person chooses to share. Explain these other terms to reinforce memory:

    ➥ **Memorial Day** — a national holiday celebrated in the United States in May to preserve the memory of soldiers who died in wars

    ➥ **memorize** — to commit to memory

    ➥ **remember** — to keep in one's memory

    ➥ **memento** — a souvenir to help a person remember an event

    ➥ **memo** — a note written as a memory aid

    ➥ **memorable** — worthy of being remembered

2. It is important for writers to remember and share significant events from their lives. This adds voice to their writing. The reader can feel that a real person has written about a real experience.

3. Have your students begin to think about writing some of their important memories in their Writer's Notebook. Use "What I Remember About…" (page 37) as a way to stir up some memories from their past. Remind them to use proper nouns for places and people to make their writing genuine. Remind them to add feeling statements. If time permits, share some of these writings in class.

4. Remind students to regularly include in their notebooks memories of important events and also of small, everyday occurrences that were meaningful in some way. Some of these might serve as story starters or provide descriptive character sketches for fiction writing.

5. Have students write their memoirs using the "What I Remember About…" page. Assemble little booklets using construction paper covers with at least 10 copy-paper pages stapled inside. Have students devote one page for each of the 10 memory prompts. They should write a brief narrative (and illustrate it, if they wish). Covers can be designed, too.

6. In small groups, have students share a page from their booklets. Suggest sincere feedback. Strongly encourage—but don't force—each group member to share a memory. You may opt to ask everyone to first share their toddler or preschool memory. These usually generate laughter, which often puts hesitant contributors at ease. These more-timid students need to learn that "laughing with" is not the same thing as "laughing at."

Lesson 10 – Saving Treasured Memories (cont.)

What I Remember About . . .

- being a toddler

  _____

  _____

- going to preschool or daycare

  _____

  _____

- my first day of elementary school

  _____

  _____

- celebrating holidays

  _____

  _____

- my birthday parties

  _____

  _____

- my best friends

  _____

  _____

- summer vacations

  _____

  _____

- special awards or recognitions

  _____

  _____

- some favorite teachers

  _____

  _____

Chapter 11 – Collecting Unique Expressions

Another feature of writing with voice is the use of certain expressions that are the author's own. In fact, sometimes readers can easily tell who is writing because they are very familiar with how that person expresses him- or herself in conversation,

Materials Needed: student copies of page 39

1. For fun, divide your class into several small groups. Instruct each group to generate a list of cartoon or TV characters or characters from literature and their famous expressions. Here are some examples: "To infinity and beyond!" (Buzz Lightyear); "What's up, Doc?" (Bugs Bunny); "Oh, bother" (Winnie-the-Pooh).

   This should be very easy for them, and they'll immediately understand that real people also can be identified by the expressions they often say or write. (Most likely, they'll even be able to connect certain phrases with certain teachers!)

2. Use "How Would You Say It?" (page 39) to help your students think about how they express themselves when talking to each other. Remind them that writing with voice means showing their personality as they "speak" on paper. Responses might include the folowing:

   ✎ "I'm so disappointed." ⟶ "I'm so bummed out."

   ✎ "I like it." ⟶ "It's totally awesome!" "It's the bomb!" "It totally rocks!"

   ✎ "I'm embarrassed." ⟶ "I feel like crawling in a hole." "My face is red."

   ✎ "I lost." ⟶ "I got creamed." "I went down." "I was denied."

   ✎ "I won." ⟶ "I aced it." "I ruled." "I came out on top."

   ✎ "I'm nervous." ⟶ "I'm so freaked out." "I'm stressed."

   ✎ "I'm hungry." ⟶ "I could eat a horse." "I'm starving."

   ✎ "I'm bored." ⟶ "This is a real yawner." "This is a snoozer."

   ✎ "I had fun." ⟶ "It was a blast." "It rocked."

3. Ask students to listen to an older person that they know and record some of his or her expressions in their Writer's Notebook. They might need these expressions for telling a story or relating a memory. For example, to say that something is really wonderful a very old person might say, "It's the cat's pajamas." Some adults might call it "groovy." Younger adults might say it's "rad" or "awesome." Knowing these expressions helps students to add voice to the characters—fictional or real—that appear in the stories they write. This is also true of people from different eras, countries, or even different regions of the same country.

4. For fun, have students orally recount a recent event at school using the voice of a pirate to retell the story. You may wish to generate a list of pirate vocabulary (such as "Ahoy, matey," "Shiver me timbers," and "Arrrrr!") beforehand.

Chapter 11 – Collecting Unique Expressions (cont.)

How Would You Say It?

✏ I'm so disappointed.

_____

✏ I like it.

_____

✏ I'm sad.

_____

✏ I'm embarrassed.

_____

✏ I lost.

_____

✏ I won.

_____

✏ I'm nervous.

_____

✏ I'm hungry.

_____

✏ I'm bored.

_____

✏ I'm sick.

_____

✏ I was surprised.

_____

✏ I had fun.

_____

* *Remember to use these expressions in your writing so your voice is heard.*

Lesson 12 – Focusing on Small Details

One mistake that young writers often make is to tackle huge, general topics and then end up doing only a mediocre job with them. Their writing would be much more powerful and their voice more evident if students learned how to focus on the small details that are often overlooked by others and tell their story instead.

Materials Needed: *a large poster (see #1), a package of cream-filled sandwich cookies (e.g., Oreo® cookies), craft sticks, yarn, rulers, student copies and transparencies of pages 42–43*

1. Locate a large poster or picture with a lot going on in it (for example, a school playground at recess).

    ✏ First, ask students to look at the poster, then give them three minutes to write a quick summary of what the whole picture is about.

    ✏ Next, have them select one detail in the picture and write for three minutes about that one detail only (for example, girls jumping rope).

    ✏ Finally, tell your students to select one small detail about that detail and spend three more minutes writing about that one tiny thing only (for example, one jumper's untied shoelace).

    Ask your students which entry was their best writing. They'll probably select the last one. Explain that their Writer's Notebooks should be full of these small details that can inspire very exact, descriptive writing.

2. Explain that writing about a small detail requires more concentration in order to pick out what is significant about it. It requires writers to concentrate on those things that typical, casual observers overlook and call these to the reader's attention. Writing about the small details forces readers to look deeper, to maybe really see something for the very first time.

3. To illustrate getting in touch with the small details, give each student a sandwich cookie and tell them to eat it right away. Next, after all the cookies have been eaten, ask the students to draw the design that was on their cookie. Probably no one will be able to do it. Now give them a second cookie and have them draw the design, adding all of its elements. Watch them do this. Notice how hard they're concentrating in order to draw it correctly. It's like they are really seeing the cookie for the first time. This is what you want in their writing. (**Note:** If you do not wish to use food to illustrate this concept, you may simply have students clear off their desks then try to draw from memory the cover of one of their textbooks.)

Lesson 12 – Focusing on Small Details (cont.)

4. To practice looking at small details, give each student 1½ yards of yarn, four craft sticks, and a ruler. Have students also bring along pencils and their notebooks. Take them outside and have each student stake out a square foot of grass using the yarn, sticks, and ruler. (Give a time limit.) Now, for about 10 minutes, have them examine their square foot of grass and write down the small details that they observe, noting colors, insect activity, rocks, etc. In class, assign a written description of their tiny piece of real estate and challenge them to write a complete page about what they observed. (An in-class alternative would be to assign one floor tile to each student and have him or her observe it closely, noting scuff marks, scratches, fading, wax build-up, etc.)

5. Use "Candy Corn Writing" (page 42) for more practice in focusing on small details. Model on a transparency by using a few examples from your Writer's Notebook. The directions are on the worksheet.

6. Sometimes when students jot down entries in their Writer's Notebook, they fail to record the pertinent details that fully describe an event. Later on, when they want to write about it, they may have forgotten this important information that would have added so much to their retelling of the story. Use "Using the 5 Ws to Add Details" (page 43) as a strategy for helping students to remember to record important details about events right when they happen—before they forget. Explain that when television, radio, and newspaper reporters are sent to cover a story, they always search out the 5 Ws. Write these on the board:

✏ Who?   ✏ Where?   ✏ Why?

✏ What?   ✏ When?

If students include these five details, then their story will be complete.

7. Distribute page 43 and work through the first example together. (You may wish to make a transparency.) Your example may look similar to this one: *I lost my sister's necklace.* This statement leaves us with a lot of questions, such as . . .

✏ **Who?** ⟶ my sister Diane

✏ **What?** ⟶ the heart necklace she got from Grandma for her 13th birthday

✏ **Where?** ⟶ at my friend's Valentine's Day party

✏ **When?** ⟶ last Saturday afternoon

✏ **Why?** ⟶ I don't think I closed the clasp completely.

Here is a possible rewrite of the original statement:

> I lost my sister Diane's heart necklace last Saturday afternoon at my friend's Valentine's Day party. She had received it as a gift from our grandma on her 13th birthday. I think it slipped off my neck because I hadn't completely closed the clasp.

Students should be able to see that details matter when writing about an event. Encourage them to record these in their Writer's Notebook immediately—perhaps using the 5 Ws strategy—so they won't forget them.

Lesson 12 – Focusing on Small Details (cont.)

Candy Corn Writing

Directions: Select four entries from your Writer's Notebook and write a quick summary of each one in the bottom section of each piece of candy corn. Now narrow the topic and write that detail in the middle section. Last, focus on one small detail of the previous detail. Write it down in the top section. Now you've learned to focus.

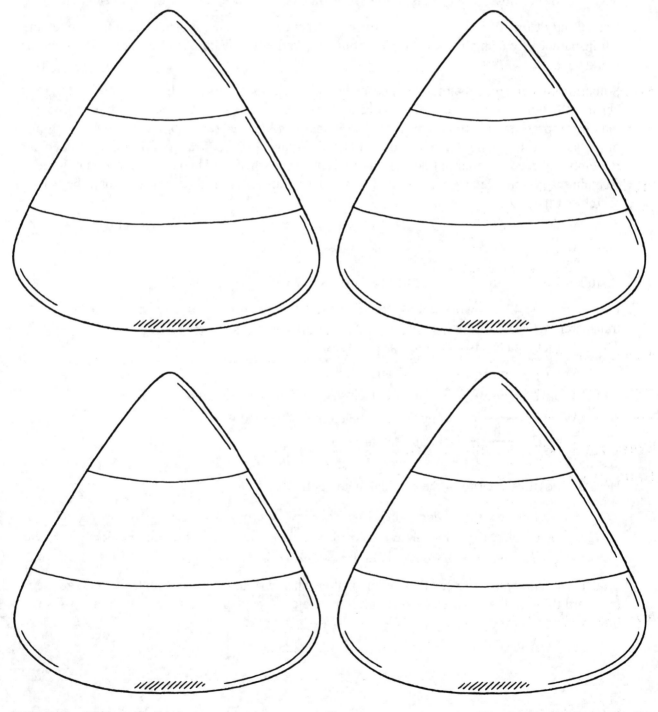

Lesson 12 – Focusing on Small Details (cont.)

Using the 5 Ws to Add Details

I lost my sister's necklace.

Elaborate on . . . ✏ Who? _____

✏ What? _____

✏ Where? _____

✏ When? _____

✏ Why? _____

Now rewrite this idea. _____

_____

_____

He loves to play video games.

Elaborate on . . . ✏ Who? _____

✏ What? _____

✏ Where? _____

✏ When? _____

✏ Why? _____

Now rewrite this idea. _____

_____

_____

Their party was so much fun.

Elaborate on . . . ✏ Who? _____

✏ What? _____

✏ Where? _____

✏ When? _____

✏ Why? _____

Now rewrite this idea. _____

_____

_____

Lesson 13 – The Computer and the Writer's Notebook

Have you ever tried to imagine what it was like for writers a long time ago? Can you imagine one of the Brontë sisters or Mark Twain completing one of their many long literary works with only a pen and paper? Can you imagine how long it must have taken to write a perfect manuscript for copying? And do you ever wonder how many more novels, sonnets, and plays William Shakespeare could have completed had he had access to word processing?

Students of today have no understanding of life without a computer. What an amazing resource it is for our young writers. With the Internet, students can access all sorts of informational websites to research facts for nonfiction writing, use Google to generate images to illustrate their work, and even download fancy stationery to publish their written pieces. Word-processing programs allow students to type their stories in the font of their choice and add special symbols or flourishes in color to make their writing stand out. And, of course, there's "spell check," the best resource of all!

Materials Needed: *a transparency of page 45*

1. Make a transparency of the Venn diagram on page 45 or draw one on the board. Explain to students that both the computer and the Writer's Notebook are important writing resources. Complete the diagram together, noting what they have in common and how they help writers differently. Students should be able to realize that both have a well-defined place in the writer's world and that they should not ignore one for the other. Responses might include the following:

The Computer:
- ✏ practice font styles and colors
- ✏ e-mail ideas or written pieces to each other for feedback
- ✏ do research to locate facts or confirm information at useful websites
- ✏ add clip art to dress up compositions
- ✏ provide a neat presentation if your handwriting is bad
- ✏ use "spell check" for accurate writing
- ✏ fix mistakes or change text around easily when composing stories or reports

The Writer's Notebook:
- ✏ use anytime, anywhere
- ✏ mobile; fits in book bag or purse
- ✏ inexpensive to make and use
- ✏ can flip through it at your desk anytime you need to without getting up
- ✏ can use during a power outage or where computers can't be used
- ✏ can use it to store clippings, drawings, pictures, and articles

Both:
- ✏ provide a place to save your ideas either on paper or in a created file
- ✏ voice can still be heard, whether on a piece of paper or a computer screen

Lesson 13 – The Computer and the Writer's Notebook (cont.)

Compatible Writing Resources

Directions: How do these resources help? Fill in the diagram.

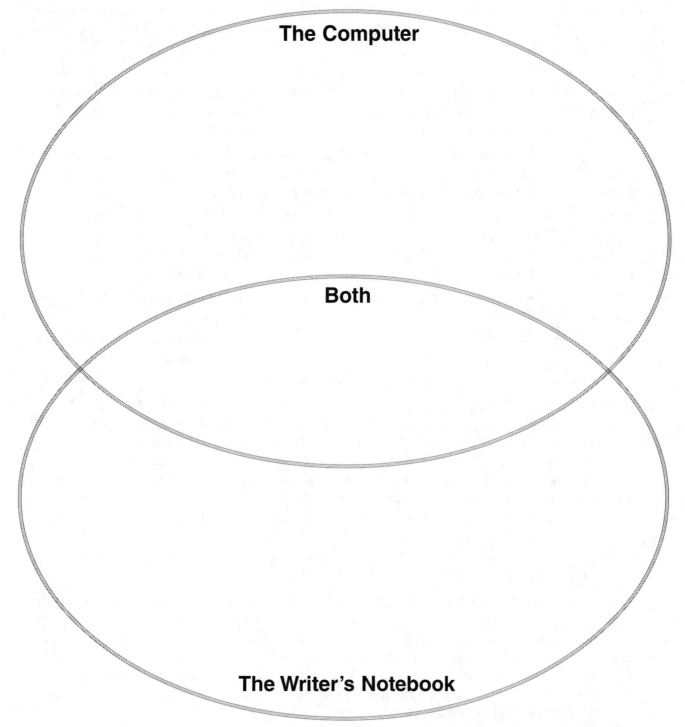

The Computer

Both

The Writer's Notebook

Lesson 14 – Revisiting and Recycling Entries

Experienced writers, both professional and amateur, never throw away a full Writer's Notebook because they're wise enough to know that a good idea is both timeless and versatile. In other words, there is no expiration date on an entry. It can be recycled and repurposed again and again. Therefore, the writer's voice can be made evident through many writing modes, often capturing a greater audience.

Materials Needed: *a cut-up file folder (as explained in #1), student copies of page 47, a transparency of page 48*

1. Ask your students if they've ever wondered why you've never told them to cross out entries in their Writer's Notebooks after they've used them one time or throw away their older notebooks. As an object lesson, show them a manila file folder that you have cut out in this way:

   Tell them that it is just one file folder but you made many things out of it. First, you cut out their Writer's Notebook covers. Then you used the leftover pieces to make bookmarks or reading place-keepers. Explain that their notebook entries are the same as the file folder. One entry can be many things, so it is important not to cross it off after just one use.

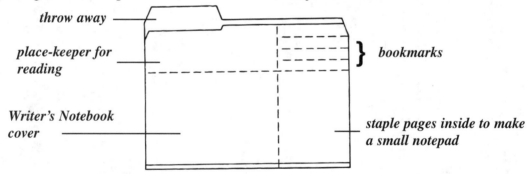

2. Use the "birdfeeder" sample on page 48 or use one of your own real entries to illustrate this concept. Carefully explain how the writer (or you) used one small entry to inspire several different types writing. Now, distribute copies of the blank "What Else Could This Be?" worksheet (page 47) and have each student select one entry from his or her notebook to use to create a short story, poem, play, and a friendly letter. Be sure to allow plenty of time. This activity may be difficult for some students—especially the first time it's practiced—so be generous with your praise and encouragement. Provide individual help but avoid giving away too many of your best ideas because the point here is for students to pull out their own ideas. Listening to other students read their examples should be very helpful, so give several students the opportunity to do this as a way to help their less-confident classmates.

3. Sometimes writers recycle an idea from their Writer's Notebook and create a new piece of writing while staying in the same genre. They can do this by changing point of view, rearranging events, or adding characters. Challenge your students to try this. Ask them to look through their Writer's Notebook and select one incident that they recorded. Instruct them to rewrite the incident from a different point of view. For instance, if a student wrote about discovering a large spider in a fuzzy slipper one morning, have them rewrite the story as being told by the spider. The story could even be written from the slipper's point of view.

Lesson 14 – Revisiting and Recycling Entries *(cont.)*

What Else Could This Be?

Directions: Select one of your Writer's Notebook entries. Write it in the box below.

Now use your entry to create four different types of writing.

a short story:

a poem:

a play:

a friendly letter:

Lesson 14 – Revisiting and Recycling Entries *(cont.)*

Sample Page

Directions: Select one of your Writer's Notebook entries. Write it in the box below.

> fun to watch the chickadees at the
> backyard birdfeeder

Now use your entry to create four different types of writing.

a short story:

THE BIRDFEEDER

We loved feeding the birds all winter, but in mid-January we had to stop. It seems that the seeds were attracting the deer. The woods are across a busy road, and we didn't want to lure them over. The choice was hard since we love both animals. It's up to nature now.

a poem:

CHICKADEES

I love you, little chickadees.
I think you mean the world to me.
I love to watch you when you eat.
Your chirping is so very sweet.
You make me smile each time you come.
When you're around, I'm never glum.

a play:

HUNGRY BIRDS

1st Bird: (in flight) I hope that family remembered to fill the birdfeeder. I'm starving!

2nd Bird: Relax! They always keep it full for us, that is, if the squirrels don't get to it first.

1st Bird: Hey! I see it and it's filled to the top. Let's eat!

a friendly letter:

Dear Family,
    Thank you for feeding us all winter. We especially loved the black sunflower seeds you gave us. They're our favorite food!
    ♡ Love,
        The Chickadees
P.S. See you this summer!

48

Lesson 15 – Collecting Useful Words and Phrases

When students are in a hurry to complete a writing assignment, they intentionally omit colorful words, figurative language, quotes, and wise sayings because, first of all, they can't think of any of these quickly, and secondly, they don't want to waste time looking up the spelling of any fancy words. In doing so, they have sacrificed those special touches that make writing memorable and a pleasure to read and more importantly they have made their voice less evident to the reader. Maintaining a "mini-mart" of these in their writer's notebooks will provide a convenient place for picking up a few of these when needed at the last minute.

Materials Needed: *transparencies of pages 50–51, student copies of pages 52–53, a copy of* Donavan's Word Jar *by Monalisa Degross (optional)*

1. Ask students to tell you what a mini-mart is. Have them name a few in your area. Ask why shoppers might go there rather than to a large supermarket. The answer would be that you can just want to run in, grab a few items, and get out quickly.

2. Now ask them to compare a mini-mart to a Writer's Notebook. Hopefully, they'll observe that both are places to get what you need quickly and conveniently. You may have to do a little searching in the "aisles," but you'll always find what you're looking for—without even leaving your desk!

3. Introduce students to "Shopping at the Mini-Mart" (page 50) as a transparency to give examples of useful words, figurative language, quotes, and wise sayings to collect. (You may need to provide definitions, as well. See page 51.) As you read stories or articles in class, be sure to point these out as they appear in the text, (Worksheets that provide practice with the use of similes and idioms are on pages 52 and 53.)

4. Whenever a student's writing seems a little dull, tell him or her that it's time to make a flying trip to their mini-mart to pick up "a tasty morsel" that will make their writing lip-smacking good. Always say this loud enough so that other students will get the message and refer to their Writer's Notebooks, as well.

5. *Optional Activity:* Third- and fourth-grade students may be familiar with *Donavan's Word Jar* by Monalisa Degross. It is the story of a boy named Donavan Allen who loves to collect interesting words like "persnickety" and "bamboozle." He writes them down and saves them in a large glass jar. The story tells the impact that his words have when his jar becomes too full to hold any more. Read this story to your students and talk about some of the words that Donavan chose to collect. Explain that a Writer's Notebook might be a more convenient way to save special words. Ask them why. You will get responses such as . . .

   ✏ A Writer's Notebook isn't as heavy as a jar.

   ✏ A Writer's Notebook can fit into your desk better.

   ✏ It's easier to locate a word in a Writer's Notebook when you need it.

   Suggest that students may want to label one page of their Writer's Notebook as "_____'s Word Jar" and use it to collect special words like Donavan did.

Lesson 15 – Collecting Useful Words and Phrases (cont.)

Shopping at the Mini-Mart

Here are some words and phrases that you can grab in a pinch:

Words

unknown words	proper nouns
interesting words	foreign words
jargon	made-up words
colorful adjectives	vivid verbs
slang words	spelling "demons"

Figurative Language

metaphors	onomatopoeia
similes	alliteration
hyperbole	idioms
personification	symbols

Quotes

from speeches	from movies
from books or stories	from conversations
from websites	from famous people
from poetry or verse	from television

Wise Sayings

from religious texts	from conversations
from books or stories	from famous people
from websites	from fables
from common use	from family tradition

Lesson 15 – Collecting Useful Words and Phrases *(cont.)*

Some Definitions You Need to Know

alliteration — repetition of the same letter or sound

Example: A <u>w</u>onderful <u>w</u>orld of <u>w</u>onders a<u>w</u>aits you.

hyperbole — an exaggeration, an overstatement for effect

Example: I've told you <u>a million times</u> to stop talking so loud.

idioms — phrases that cannot be taken literally

Example: "so hungry I could eat a horse," "get on the ball," "hop to it"

jargon — specific vocabulary used by some professionals

Example: Computer techs use such jargon as "download," "RAM," and "bytes."

metaphors — making a direct comparison between two things (often using "is" or "was")

Example: Each new day <u>is</u> a gift.

onomatopoeia — words that sound like the noises they describe

Example: "swoosh," "crash," "tinkle," "buzz"

personification — giving human qualities to something non-living

Example: The sun <u>smiled</u> on us.

similes — using the words "like" or "as" to compare two things

Example: "as pretty <u>as</u> a picture," "shook <u>like</u> an earthquake"

slang — common, informal expressions that oftentimes go out of style quickly

Example: "far out," "groovy," "cool"

symbols — something that stands for more than what it is

Example: The Statue of Liberty means freedom.

Lesson 15 – Collecting Useful Words and Phrases *(cont.)*

Simile Practice

Directions: Complete each sentence using a simile.

Example: My teacher is as <u>energetic</u> as <u>an Olympic runner</u>.

My Teacher

My teacher is as _____ as _____.

His/her hair is as _____ as _____.

His/her eyes are as _____ as _____.

His/her smile is as _____ as _____.

His/her laugh is as _____ as _____.

His/her desk is as _____ as _____.

At School

My school is as _____ as _____.

My classroom is as _____ as _____.

Recess is as _____ as _____.

Field trips are as _____ as _____.

Report cards can be as _____ as _____.

Cafeteria food is as _____ as _____.

My classmates are as _____ as _____.

My desk is as _____ as _____.

When I write, I am as _____ as _____.

Me

My eyes are as _____ as _____.

My nose is as _____ as _____.

My hair is as _____ as _____.

My hands are as _____ as _____.

My feet are as _____ as _____.

My fingernails are as _____ as _____.

My teeth are as _____ as _____.

Today I'm as _____ as _____.

Lesson 15 – Collecting Useful Words and Phrases *(cont.)*

Illustrate Those Idioms

Directions: Idioms are figurative expressions that should not be taken literally. Draw a line to match the idioms on the left to their figurative meanings on the right.

I'm on pins and needles.	got mad at me
Don't pull my leg.	easy to do
Now hold your horses!	very nervous
Let's get the ball rolling.	pay bills
Bill jumped down my throat.	tease me
She's wet behind the ears.	get started
I'm on cloud nine.	new at this
This will be a piece of cake.	really happy
It's hard to make ends meet.	took a chance
He stuck his neck out.	wait a minute

Directions: Now have fun. Choose four of these idioms and draw them literally. Be sure to label each one.

Chapter 3

Teaching Students to Live Like Writers

Introduction

Ask students to describe the lifestyle of some famous celebrity, and they'll easily be able to tell about his or her extravagant parties, shopping sprees, trips down the red carpet at award ceremonies, and run-ins with the paparazzi. But if you asked students to describe the lifestyle of some famous author, they might be hard-pressed to describe just how they live, except for guessing that they must spend enormous amounts of time alone, hunched in front of a computer screen.

Except for maybe J.K. Rowling, very few authors of children's books make the national (or world) news. Very few appear on popular syndicated talk shows, and children who have read sets of books by one particular author generally have no idea where that author lives and how he or she produces books for publication. So when you challenge your students to live like writers, to adopt the writer's lifestyle as their own, they have little idea what that is. In fact, it might sound a little boring to them—certainly not glamorous.

You must use the Writer's Notebook as a way for students to begin to understand how writers practice their craft. As they learn to rely on this resource as an essential storehouse for collecting ideas, they'll begin to sense how writers effectively prepare to organize and then compose their written pieces.

Possibly one of the best things you could do for your students is to invite an author to visit your school. Of course, this may be easier said than done, depending on where you live and the financial resources available, but check with your public library. They may be aware of local authors (perhaps as yet unpublished) who would be willing to visit your school at no cost as a way to promote their work. If you are lucky enough to snag such an author, make sure that your students prepare well in advance for his or her visit.

Work as a class (or school) to plan hospitality details, create a schedule of presentations (if visiting more than one classroom), and plan publicity for the event. Students should read portions of the visitor's book in advance and prepare comments and brainstorm questions. They might want to ask the author where he or she got the idea for the book, what kind of research was necessary, who drew the pictures or took the photographs, how long it took to write the book, and whether or not there will be more books written,

One question that students should also ask is if the author keeps a Writer's Notebook. (You might want to check this out ahead of time.) Your students may be eager to show off their notebooks or some of their stories and ask for feedback. Hopefully, your visiting author will accommodate your writers and celebrate their efforts—and maybe even offer some helpful advice. And now that they have finally met a real live author, your students might want to maintain some sort of ongoing relationship, perhaps through e-mail, as a way to better understand writing as a profession. How exciting would that be?

Lesson 16 – The Writer's Muse

One of the hardest things for young writers to learn is how to wait quietly and patiently for inspiration. This is the perfect age to introduce them to their very own Muse.

Materials Needed: *a world map, student copies of page 56, a transparency of page 57*

---

1. Explain that a very long time ago in the country of Greece (show this on a map), the people who lived there believed in many gods and goddesses. Zeus was the king of all gods. Athena was the goddess of wisdom. Poseidon was the god of the ocean. Aphrodite was the goddess of love. The Greeks had hundreds of them! There was also a group of nine goddesses who were the goddesses of inspiration. They were called the Muses. From their name, we get several words:

   ✏ *museum* — the dwelling place of the Muses, a public display of creativity

   ✏ *amusement* — entertainment of the creative or inspired mind

   ✏ *musings* — inspired thoughts, wonderings, or reflections

   There was a Muse who inspired musicians, one who inspired artists, and another who inspired actors. Several of the Muses inspired writers. It was believed that a writer could only write when his own personal Muse whispered creative thoughts in his ear. In other words, she was inspiration personified.

2. *Personification* means giving a non-living thing the identity or characteristics of a real person. Jack Frost, Mother Nature, Old Man Winter, and Father Time are modern-day examples of how we sometimes personify natural occurrences. We might say, "Mother Nature sure has given us a beautiful day" or "Old Man Winter came early this year." Since a Muse is inspiration personified, we might say, "I couldn't come up with an idea for a story until my Muse visited me." In other words, I couldn't write until I was inspired.

3. Explain that a Writer's Notebook is there to hold our musings as they happen. In them we record what we wonder about, question, or reflect on.

4. Practice musing with "Classroom Musings" (page 56). Show the sample (page 57) as a transparency, then remove it from view. Tell your students that you are going to allow plenty of time for their Muses to "visit them" as they write down their thoughts while looking at each object. Take time to share musings.

5. Explain that writers sometimes get stuck. We call it "writer's block." It's when we just can't seem to get an idea. Whenever this happens, we need to call on our Muse for inspiration. How do we do this? By quietly observing the world around us, keeping our minds open to new ideas, and patiently waiting for our writing juices to flow.

6. If you are an especially fun-loving teacher, at times dress up in a sheet that is wrapped toga-style. Do this whenever the class as a whole seems unmotivated to write. Frolic and flit around the classroom (maybe to a recording of harp music) and whisper ideas into the ears of students who need your visit to inspire them. They'll love it, and you'll create a lifetime memory. They may even suggest when it's time for you to appear.

Lesson 16 – The Writer's Muse (cont.)
Classroom Musings

What I sometimes wonder about . . .

✏ **our country's flag**

_____

_____

_____

_____

✏ **our clock**

_____

_____

_____

_____

✏ **my desk**

_____

_____

_____

_____

✏ **our whiteboard/chalkboard**

_____

_____

_____

_____

✏ **my classmates**

_____

_____

_____

_____

Lesson 16 – The Writer's Muse (cont.)

Sample Page

What I sometimes wonder about . . .

✏ **our country's flag**

Every morning we are told to face the flag and say the pledge, but I wonder if I'm in the hall at that time, where should I look to say the pledge. I guess you just put your hand over your heart, close your eyes, and pretend it's there. That's still patriotic.

✏ **our clock**

Whenever I look at the clock, it makes me wonder about kids in school a long time ago. How could teachers mark students tardy? How did they know when it was lunchtime? or recess? or dismissal? Maybe they just waited until they were hungry, restless, or tired.

✏ **my desk**

I wonder how many kids have had this desk before me. I wonder if my older brother sat here. If he did, I bet this desk was always messy. I'm very neat, so I think this desk is lucky to have me sitting here this year. I never scratch or mark on it.

✏ **our whiteboard/chalkboard**

Every time I look at the whiteboard I think about how much fun it would be to have one in my bedroom at home. I could practice math facts and play Tic-tac-toe or Hangman with my sisters. I could draw on it too. That's what I'd mostly do, I think.

✏ **my classmates**

Sometimes I wonder what we'll all look like as grown-ups. Will Josh and Benjamin have beards? Will any of us be famous? Will all of us get married? Who knows? Maybe one day one of us will be president, then we can say that we went to school together.

Lesson 17 – A Time for Self-Evaluation

It is important for all of us to step back now and then to reflect on certain aspects of our lives. Students should be taught to do this regularly as a way to get in touch with themselves as writers. They should be able to look at finished pieces of their writing and determine both strengths and weaknesses. They should first solicit and then reflect on honest feedback given by teachers and fellow classmates. Most importantly, they need to identify what it is that they feel most passionate about and decide how they will share this passion convincingly with their readers.

Materials Needed: *student copies of page 59*

1. Occasionally show students one of your well-written letters or essays and emphasize how proud you are of it. Then show them some of your first attempts all wadded up. Remind them that writing is a process of trial and error. Tell them that pencils aren't made with erasers on one end because manufacturers *think* you might make mistakes—they *know* you'll make mistakes! A lot of them! Everyone does. That's why packages of just eraser tips are also sold.

2. Distribute "Myself as a Writer" (page 59) and ask students to thoughtfully respond to each question.

3. This is a great opportunity for students to support and learn from each other. Divide your class into groups of three to five and have them review "Myself as a Writer" as a Share and Compare time. Circulate around the room to make sure that every student is contributing.

4. Don't miss this opportunity to evaluate yourself as a writing teacher. Ask these questions:

    - Have I created a comfortable writing environment for my students?
    - Have I shown my students that there is value in their ideas?
    - Do I look for opportunities to remind students to record their ideas?
    - Have I helped my students find their voice?
    - Do I see evidence of voice in their writing?
    - Have I introduced them to writing as a life-long, pleasurable activity?
    - Am I keeping my own Writer's Notebook?
    - Is my love of writing evident? Do I see it in my students?

5. Write this quote on the board. Ask students what they think it means.

    " . . . write things worth reading or do things worth writing."
    — *Benjamin Franklin*

Does this have to be a choice? Couldn't a writer do both? Certainly! A good writer should try to experience many things, then write about those experiences in such a way that readers will be informed and/or motivated to experience them, too. Challenge your students to enthusiastically experience life, then grab their Writer's Notebooks and fill them full!

Lesson 17 – A Time for Self-Evaluation (cont.)

Myself as a Writer

1. When given a choice, how do I decide what to write about?

_____

_____

2. What do I like to write about the most? Why?

_____

_____

3. Who has had the most influence on the way I write?

_____

_____

4. Which author's style would I most like to copy?

_____

_____

5. What is the best thing I've ever written?

_____

_____

6. What writing genre do I most often avoid? Why?

_____

_____

7. Am I usually proud of what I write?

_____

_____

8. Who do I usually trust to give me honest feedback?

_____

_____

9. What goals can I set for myself as a writer?

_____

_____

10. Writing in general: "thumbs up" or "thumbs down"?

_____

_____

Lesson 18 – Learning from Other Writers

Wouldn't it be wonderful if every aspiring writer had a successful, professional writer as a mentor? Well they can, simply by opening one of their books and paying close attention to what that author did to make his or her book so memorable.

Materials Needed: *none*

1. When we are reading a fictional book, we usually focus on the characters and the action of the story, and we rarely think about just what the author is doing to hold our attention so effectively. (Write these on the board or overhead as you explain them.)

    To engage a reader, a writer can use . . .

    - ✎ **Setting Description** — Detailed descriptions of periods in history, various groups of people, and geographic locations (both imaginary and real), are described so completely that the reader feels like part of the action.

    - ✎ **Character Development** — Characters are described with such care that readers are able to predict what they will do next or how they will feel throughout the story. The reader is able to make personal connections when sharing a character's joy, fear, sorrow, or excitement.

    - ✎ **Plot Development** — The story line is developed in such a way as to capture the reader's complete attention as events unfold and the story reaches an exciting climax, before concluding with a satisfying, sometimes surprising, ending.

    - ✎ **Figurative Language** — Similes, metaphors, and idioms dress up writing. Colloquialisms and slang make it sound familiar and comfortable to read.

    - ✎ **Humor** — Characters are given humorous dialogue, and certain events in the story line may include a comical twist. These elements keep the reader entertained throughout and make the story memorable.

    - ✎ **Interesting Fact**s — Facts are presented clearly, concisely, logically, and in a manner that provides a sense of realism and is relevant to the story.

2. The Writer's Notebook is a safe place for beginning writers to try out some of these literary elements, but first they need to locate examples from literature to judge the effectiveness of each one. They need to determine why an author chose to use that particular element to help tell their story and how skillful they were in doing so.

3. Organize literature scavenger hunts. Divide your class into six groups and put each group in charge of one of the six literary elements (e.g., one group has setting description, one has character development, and so on). After each story is read from the basal reading series, have each group report on how well they feel the author employed the assigned literary element. Have each group use a score of 1 ("Weak or Nonexistent Use"), 2 ("Some Use"), or 3 ("Awesome Use!") to rate the author's use of the element. This will show which elements are more commonly employed by authors to engage readers and which are most effective.

Lesson 18 – Learning from Other Writers (cont.)

4. Use this activity as an opportunity to suggest to your students that perhaps these authors used a Writer's Notebook to collect examples of these literary elements. They should be doing this, too.

5. Now that your students have learned about some ways that writers engage readers, it's a good time to think about some lessons that they may have learned from reading books by several familiar authors. On the board or overhead, brainstorm a list of your students' favorite authors. Then ask your students this question: What did you learn about writing from this author?

Answers, of course, will vary, but a typical list might look like this one:

- ✎ **R.L. Stine** — It's okay to stick with one genre if you're really good at it.
- ✎ **Dr. Seuss** — It's all right to make up words when you write.
- ✎ **Laura Ingalls Wilder** — A person should remember the past in case you might want to write about it later.
- ✎ **J.K. Rowling** — If your first book is popular, you may be asked to write sequels.
- ✎ **Shel Silverstein** — Having a sense of humor is very important when you write poems.
- ✎ **Beverly Cleary** — Writing about everyday happenings can be very interesting.

6. In your classroom you might want to display a chart similar to this one:

Analyzing the Authors

Author's Name	Book/Story Title	What We Can Learn About Writing from this Author

After each story in the basal reader (or any other story shared together in class), ask the students to help you rate that author. What did they learn about how the author wrote? What literary elements did the author use? (If the reading selection is a nonfiction piece, students might suggest that the use of illustrations or charts helped to explain ideas.)

Lesson 19 – Sharing from the Writer's Notebook

Few things are sadder than a library book that has never been checked out. It's like an unopened birthday gift or an unclaimed winning lottery ticket. It's like a play presented to an empty theater or a newly built home that is standing empty.

Young writers are often so afraid of ridicule that they shy away from sharing their writing. As teachers, it is up to us to create a classroom environment that is comfortable, non-judgmental, and most of all accepting of each other's attempts at revealing their innermost thoughts on paper. Students should be eager to welcome others into their private world that is hidden in the pages of their Writer's Notebook.

Materials Needed: *none*

1. The most effective way to teach risk-taking with writing is by modeling. When the time seems right—and only you can be the judge of that—tell your students that you recently made an entry into your Writer's Notebook and that you would like to share it with them to get their opinion of the subject matter. Take great care to read an entry that is poignant and relatively easy for them to discuss. Don't shy away from serious entries like the death of a family member or a pet or revealing some problem that you've been trying to resolve. When you read, be as expressive as possible. Your students will accept your writing as genuine if you are genuine in your presentation. Afterwards, listen carefully to their insights and thank each contributor for being honest.

2. Now instruct students to look through their notebooks and pick out one special entry they'd like to share, either with one other student or in a small group. Divide the class accordingly and allow enough time for each writer to contribute. Don't force any student to share. It's a matter of trust, and group dynamics may affect a student's decision to remain silent.

3. While the process is taking place, observe the listeners. What comments are they making? Are they being supportive and sincere? Does the reader seem proud to present his or her ideas to the group? Intervene only when you feel it is necessary.

4. You might also like to try a whole-class "Reading into the Circle." Have students sit in a circle. Instruct every one to sit quietly; and when a student feels motivated, he or she should read an entry so that all can hear. Listeners may give a thumbs-up or nod, but no words can be spoken. Then the next student reads an entry. Explain that if two readers begin reading at the same time, one should politely relinquish the circle to the other and read later. End the activity when no one else chooses to read. Be sure to thank both the readers and the listeners.

Lesson 20 – Challenging Students to Live Like Writers

Authors live their passion every day, every hour. If they are not writing, they are quietly observing their world and waiting for a visit from their Muse.

Materials Needed: *student copies of page 64*

1. Write these seven words on the board in front of the class: *Observe, Connect, Experience, Write, Imitate, Practice, Self-Evaluate.* Have these words displayed as you explain each of the concepts. Explain that real writers engage in certain activities that will serve them a lifetime. Writers . . .

   ✏ **Observe** — Writers are always aware of the world around them. They look at details big and small.

   ✏ **Connect** — Writers make connections to what they hear, see, and read.

   ✏ **Experience** — Writers get out and experience life so they can write about it. They have real stories to share with their readers.

   ✏ **Write** — Writers write daily and keep their Writer's Notebook handy to jot down ideas and record their experiences.

   ✏ **Imitate** — Writers read extensively as a way to experience various styles of writing that they may want to try, as well.

   ✏ **Practice** — Writers take risks with their writing by exploring new subjects and trying unfamiliar genres. They are willing to practice difficult skills.

   ✏ **Self-evaluate** — Writers always take time to reflect on their craft. They share their writing with others to get honest, constructive feedback.

   Distribute copies of "How to Live Like a Writer" (page 64) as a resource for your students.

2. Have each student select a favorite author to research on the Internet. Ask them to look for examples of how they observe, connect, experience, etc. Have students present their findings in oral reports to the class so comparisons can be noted.

3. Teach your students this poem:

   > Good, better, best
   >
   > Never let it rest
   >
   > 'Til your good gets better,
   >
   > And your better gets BEST!
   >
   > — *author unknown*

Recite this poem often as encouragement. Display it in the classroom. Have students copy it in their Writer's Notebook and commit it to memory.

Lesson 20 – Challenging Students to Live Like Writers *(cont.)*

How to Live Like a Writer

1. Write every day.

   - Find a quiet, comfortable place to write.

   - Set aside a certain time to write each day. Make it a habit!

   - Ask parents and siblings to respect your privacy as you write.

2. Make your Writer's Notebook a constant companion.

   - Keep your notebook in a safe place along with a pen or pencil.

   - Save all filled notebooks. Review them often for ideas.

3. Read as many books as you can.

   - Read both fiction and nonfiction. Trade books with friends.

   - Leave your reading comfort zone. Tackle books that typically you wouldn't read. Venture into other genres.

4. Talk to many people and listen to what they have to say. Keep an open mind.

   - Talk to people of all ages, backgrounds, and interests.

   - Ask older adults to tell how life was long ago.

5. Summon your Muse for inspiration.

   - Write about the things that are the most important to you.

6. Keep a list of new or interesting words or phrases.

   - Buy a small dictionary. Keep it handy.

   - Underline new words as you read to look up later. (Use a notepad to copy the words in if the book isn't yours.)

7. Celebrate your efforts.

   - Find people who you trust, and then share your writing with them. Listen to them as they share their writing with you.

   - Encourage others to give you honest feedback, and do the same for them.

8. View yourself as "a writer," because YOU ARE!